IN THEIR OWN WORDS

WORLD WAR I

A Primary Source History

Nicholas Saunders

GARETH**STEVENS**
GS
PUBLISHING
A Member of the WRC Media Family of Companies

KEY TO SYMBOLS
The following symbols highlight the sources of material from the past.

FILM EXCERPT
Primary source material from a movie about the subject matter.

SONG EXCERPT/POEM
Text from songs or poems about the subject matter.

OFFICIAL SPEECH
Transcribed words from official government and other speeches.

GOVERNMENT DOCUMENT
Text from an official government document.

LETTER
Text from a letter written by a participant in the events.

PLAQUE/INSCRIPTION
Text from plaques or monuments erected in memory of events in this book.

INTERVIEW/BOOK EXTRACT
Text from an interview or book.

NEWSPAPER ARTICLE
Extracts from newspapers of the period.

TELEGRAM
Text from a telegram sent to or by a participant in the events.

Cover photos:

Top: *General Paul von Hindenburg commanded the German Eighth Army on the eastern front. Following his military career, he became president of the post-war Weimar Republic in 1925. His decision to appoint Nazi leader Adolf Hitler as chancellor of Germany proved to be a fateful one for Germany—and the world.*

Bottom: *Allied troops shown in trenches. World War I brought new military technologies and trench warfare together to create a new and brutal form of war.*

CONTENTS

Above: A map of the Balkans region (top); and (above) a map of the world before the outbreak of war. Britain's colonies are shown in pink. (Italy and Turkey are not part of the Balkans.)

Below: A gas mask and other weapons used in the war. World War 1 marked the first use of such sophisticated weapons.

World War I changed the world and produced an unbridgable divide between prewar civilization and the new, harsher existence that followed. Also called the "Great War," World War I created the modern world in which we live today. European nations had shaped and controlled countries all around the world for several hundred years. British, French, German, Dutch, Spanish, and Portuguese explorers helped settle, conquer, and colonize India, the Americas, the Middle East, and parts of Africa and Asia. Before 1914, the economic might of Britain and France and the imperial powers of Europe—royal families that were the focus of loyalty and tradition and which were closely linked with each other—dominated the world. Strong naval power helped these countries govern and maintain their far-off territories.

By the end of the nineteenth century, the developed world had been shaped by European civilization and its scientific and technological superiority. One of the great ironies of World War I was that this same technology was used against the countries that had designed it. Not only was World War I (WWI) the first global or worldwide conflict, but it was also a bitterly destructive European civil war. By its end, Europe's royal families had lost much of their influence, and new nations had emerged. WWI was also known as the Great War, because people believed that war on such a large scale would never happen again. Injustices committed during and after

WWI created resentment that eventually led to a second, even more destructive and terrible world war in 1939.

By the time of the outbreak of WWI, weaponry had advanced to a point where humans could kill and wound each other on a scale not previously imaginable. Politicians and generals, whose experiences of war up until then had been in far smaller nineteenth-century conflicts, did not grasp the implications of the new weapons they possessed. Their failure to understand these developments led to horrific numbers of wounded and dead at such battles as the Somme and Verdun (both in France) in 1916, and at Ieper (Ypres), and nearby Passchendaele, Belgium, in 1914, 1915, and 1917. It also led to unknown numbers of missing whose bodies were never found.

The Great War was also different in the way that it affected civilians. Foreign visitors caught by the outbreak of war in what had become an enemy country overnight were incarcerated in

Above: *A French poster illustrates the use of modern aircraft during the conflict.*

Below: *Archduke Franz Ferdinand (left) walks with Kaiser Wilhelm of Germany.*

Left: *A soldier in the British Royal Naval Division relaxes. The Division fought in many of the major battles, including at the Somme in France.*

5

Above: *Archduke Ferdinand and his wife, Sophie, in their car just moments before his assassination on June 28, 1914. This act is usually considered the spark that set off the tinderbox of smoldering tensions among various nations and national groups prior to World War I.*

internment camps. Across mainland Europe, civilians were forced to become refugees as the war stagnated into four years of trench warfare on the western and eastern fronts.

The conflict changed the nature and balance of international relations and military capabilities. When it began, aviation was in its infancy; the Wright Brothers' first powered flight had taken place in North Carolina less than eleven years earlier. Aircraft soon became a central feature of modern warfare. Aviation technology allowed aerial "dogfights" between opposing squadrons and aerial bombing raids. It also contributed to rapid development in camera and radio technology used in reconnaissance and communications. Similarly, the pre-war world had been dominated by hugely expensive navies. Between 1914 and 1918, Germany developed the "*Unterseeboot*"— submarines that made the older navies largely

Above: *A poster urges men to join the United States armed forces.*

Right: *The United States' entry into the war tilted the odds toward the Allies and led to Germany's surrender on November 11, 1918.*

obsolete. Explosive shells, machine guns, tanks, and the use of poisonous gases were all perfected during WWI. The nature of war changed permanently.

World War I also made a deep impression on society and culture. More women entered the workforce and became aware of a new way of life. British women won the right to vote in 1919; U.S. women followed in 1920. A large portion of an entire generation of young men died, and many more returned from war shell-shocked or maimed. Directly after WWI, the world experienced a short period of prosperity, in what became known as the "Roaring Twenties." People wanted to have fun after four years of gloom. The fun did not last long. The collapse of the financial markets on Wall Street in New York City in 1929 led to the Great Depression of the 1930s, an era of worldwide economic downturn. The world was also different politically. The map of Europe had been redrawn. Germany was humiliated by the terms of the Treaty of Versailles. This resentment helped lead to the outbreak of World War II in 1939.

The Great War dramatically changed people's ideas about the world. It also left behind an ironic legacy of war because the conflict was at first labeled "the war to end all wars."

Above: *World War I left a powerful legacy that lasted for decades. The Berlin Wall that split Berlin, Germany—though not a direct result of WWI—was among the more tangible symbols of the ongoing division between East and West. People celebrated when the Wall came down in 1989 and Berlin was reunited.*

Below: *The Battle of Lorette in northern France lasted from October 1914 to October 1915. More than one hundred thousand died. The military cemetery there contains more than twenty thousand graves.*

Above: *George V became the king of England in 1910, a reign that saw the country involved in a world war.*

The course and consequences of World War I are well known, but it is more difficult to understand why it began and why it involved so many nations. Its many causes include the political instability in the part of Europe known as the Balkans, treaties that connected one country to another, and rivalry between different countries. The lack of imagination of the politicians, members of royalty, and generals—all of whom failed to foresee the consequences of a war on such a grand scale—added to the problem.

> "I have frequently been astonished to hear with what composure and how glibly Members, and even Ministers, talk of a European war. . . . [such a conflict would end] . . . in the ruin of the vanquished and the scarcely less fatal commercial dislocation and exhaustion of the conquerors . . . The wars of peoples will be more terrible than those of kings."
>
> **Winston Churchill warned Parliament on May 13, 1901, that future wars would be different from previous ones.**

EUROPEAN ROYALTY AND MONEY

The Great War was in many respects a European civil war. It was also a war between different branches of Europe's royal houses. Russia's Czar Nicholas II and Germany's Kaiser Wilhelm II—as well as others—were related. They appeared together in a famous family photograph with Queen Victoria. Half German herself, the queen had married the German Prince Albert of Saxe-Coburg-Gotha. At the outbreak of war, 28 percent of the Germans studying at Oxford University in England were members of the German aristocracy. The worlds of finance and business were also linked, and the leading London banking families, the Rothschilds and the Kleinworts, were of German origin. These royal and financial connections and self-interest meant that Europe was ruled by different branches of the same extended royal family. It was clear to many that any European war that would shake these thrones would be best avoided.

BALKAN TINDERBOX

By 1914, the Balkan region of Eastern Europe was a time bomb

Right: *A lavish banquet was held at Buckingham Palace for Queen Victoria's Golden Jubilee. All of the crowned heads of Europe were invited. Some would be at war with each other a few years later.*

waiting to explode. The most important regional power was the multiethnic Austro-Hungarian empire based in Vienna, Austria. Its fifty million people were a volatile mix of ethnic groups, each vying for various degrees of independence and territorial claims. In 1908, the empire annexed (incorporated) both Bosnia and Herzegovina, a majority of whose population shared their language and culture with Serbia. When Germany showed support for the expansion of Austria–Hungary, Serbian and Russian resistance to the annexation faded.

0 100 200 km
0 100 200 miles

RUSSIA

Vienna
AUSTRIA–HUNGARY
Budapest
Hungarians

Dniester River
Pruth River

Hungarians

Transylvania

ROMANIA

Sava River

BOSNIA
Sarajevo
Herzegovina

Belgrade

Bucharest
Danube River

SERBIA

MONTENEGRO
Sofia

BULGARIA

Black Sea

Macedonians

Constantinople

ITALY

ALBANIA

GREECE

OTTOMAN EMPIRE

Ottoman Empire (Turkey)
Predominantly Serbs and Croats
Predominantly Romanians

Above and right: *The region of Europe dominated by the Austro-Hungarian empire in the early 1900s.*

Right: *Baroness Betty de Rothschild, part of the famous banking family living in London, was of German descent. There were many links between the two countries before war broke out.*

Complicating matters further, Bulgaria, Greece, Montenegro, and Serbia joined forces to win various other territories in the region. Austria and Italy intervened, however, and created an independent Albania. When Serbia and Bulgaria went to war in 1913, Bulgaria lost territory as a result. By June 1914, the Balkan

TIME LINE
1900–1912

1900
Germany out-produces British steel production and emerges as a major industrial power and rival to Britain.

May 13, 1901
Winston Churchill warns Parliament of the unrecognized dangers of a European war.

1906
Britain launches HMS *Dreadnought*, a new class of battleship.

1908
Austria-Hungary annexes Bosnia and Herzegovina.

1912
First Balkan War; Serbia victorious over Turkey.

"...a European war is bound to come sooner or later...[preparing]... for that contingency is the duty of all... which...champion... Germanic ideas and culture."

Helmuth von Moltke, chief of the German Imperial General Staff, speaking to General Conrad von Hötzendorf, the Austrian chief of staff, on February 10, 1913.

Above: Built in 1906, the British battleship HMS *Dreadnought* was the largest ship of its kind in the world.

Above: Count Ferdinand von Zeppelin, creator of the first fleet of zeppelin airships.

more munitions brought women into the labor force and so involved large numbers of civilians. Other new weapons of mass killing included poisonous gas and machine guns. Also, WWI saw the development of aerial bombardment from airplanes and German zeppelins. This innovation was another factor that led to the concept of "total war"—war that involved entire nations.

Air raids were frequently aimed at civilian targets, especially in Britain. The British military developed the world's first tank, and the Germans perfected submarine warfare. These new technologies changed the face of war. New military thinking was needed to take advantage of it.

region was unstable because of nationalism, rivalry between people from different ethnic groups, and political dissent.

THE WEAPONS OF TOTAL WAR

The Great War was the first global, industrialized conflict, the consequences of which were not really understood when hostilities began. Although artillery used during the U.S. Civil War inflicted severe casualties, the sheer scale of WWI bombardments using millions of shells proved deadly on a massive scale. The need to make more and

THE MOST POWERFUL NAVY IN THE WORLD

Admiral Horatio Nelson won a major victory for Britain against the French at the Battle of Trafalgar in 1805. Since then, Britain's Royal Navy had commanded the world's oceans, helping to forge and maintain the empire created during the reign of Queen Victoria from

"The news continues to be good, the Tanks seem to have done good work and fairly put the wind up the Hun who was seen to run like Hell in front of them shouting, 'This isn't war, it is murder.' For once in the war, we come into the field with a new engine of war and not second-hand copied from the Hun."

Major H. E. Trevor, 37th Infantry Brigade, wrote to his parents from the Somme River battle area on September 16, 1916, about the role of tanks. No new weapon captured the essence of industrialized war better than the tank.

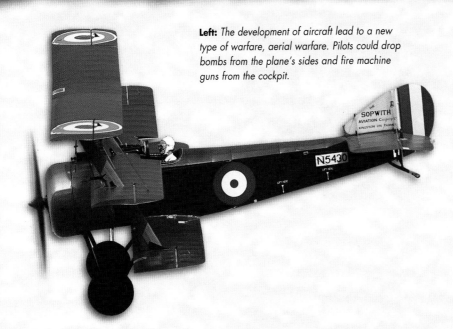

Left: *The development of aircraft lead to a new type of warfare, aerial warfare. Pilots could drop bombs from the plane's sides and fire machine guns from the cockpit.*

TIME LINE
1913–1914

1913
Second Balkan War; Germany's standing army reaches 544,000 men.

July 29, 1914
Czar Nicholas II sends telegram to Kaiser Wilhelm asking him to avoid war.

1838 to 1901. Between then and 1914, no other country dared oppose Britain's enormous and intimidating naval power. Naval technology had changed, and battleships were built of steel instead of wood. They were powered by steam rather than sails, and explosive shells had replaced cannonballs. The HMS *Dreadnought,* launched in 1906, had revolutionized battleship design with its thick armor plating and massive firepower. These new developments had never been tested in full-scale battle. Between 1898 and 1900, German Admiral

Alfred von Tirpitz developed the so-called "Tirpitz Plan" to build a high seas fleet that could challenge the Royal Navy's mastery of the oceans and thus Britain's empire.

ASSASSINATION IN SARAJEVO

On June 28, 1914, Archduke Ferdinand, the heir to the Austro-Hungarian throne, and a critic of Serbian nationalism, was visiting Sarajevo, Bosnia. Austro-Hungary had made political demands on Serbia which had not been fully met.

Above: *Submarines "came of age" during WWI. German U-boats sank at least three hundred twenty-five merchant ships during the war.*

Left *The use of machine guns during WWI helped to dramatically escalate the number of casualties.*

"In April 1916, Polly, a workmate of mine, and myself decided we would get a job on munitions. After some controversy about my age, I was only seventeen . . . I was taken on as an overhead crane driver. . . . My first impression was sheer fright, rows and rows of 8-inch, 6-inch and 9-inch shells, not forgetting the 12-inch which reached to my waist and higher . . . We were on eight-hour shifts. . . but this was changed to twelve hours . . ."

Seventeen-year old Lottie Wiggins recalls starting work in a munitions factory.

Above: *Archduke Franz Ferdinand (left) was shot dead by Bosnian Serb Gavrilo Princip.*

THE SCHLIEFFEN PLAN

Named after the German military strategist Count Alfred von Schlieffen (1833–1913), the Schlieffen Plan was designed to enable Germany to fight on two fronts. The idea was that Russia's slow mobilization would give time for a huge German force to storm through Belgium, thereby outflanking the more heavily defended French border further south. Paris would fall quickly, dealing the French army's morale a lethal blow. Germany would then send reinforcements east to confront the Russians.

Ferdinand was assassinated by eighteen-year-old Bosnian Serb student Gavrilo Princip a member of the Serbian nationalist group "Black Hand." In response, on July 28, Austro-Hungary, supported by its ally, Germany, declared war on Serbia. On July 29, Serbia's ally, Russia, began mobilizing troops against Austro-Hungary, thus also threatening Germany. On August 1, Germany declared war on Russia. On August 3, Germany invaded Russia's ally, France, and its tiny neighbor, Luxembourg. On August 4, Germany also invaded Belgium.

> "She had literally been blown to fragments. The floor, the walls, the ceilings were splotched with—well, it's enough to say that the woman's remains could only have been collected with a shovel."

On August 25, 1914, a German zeppelin airship dropped bombs on the Belgian port of Antwerp, killing Belgian citizens in their own houses. U.S. newspaper correspondent E. Alexander Powell wrote about what happened to a woman killed in her home.

Right: *Alfred von Tirpitz introduced the First Fleet Act in 1898, and a Second Fleet Act in 1900. The Acts outlined a principle of building a German navy to rival Britain's.*

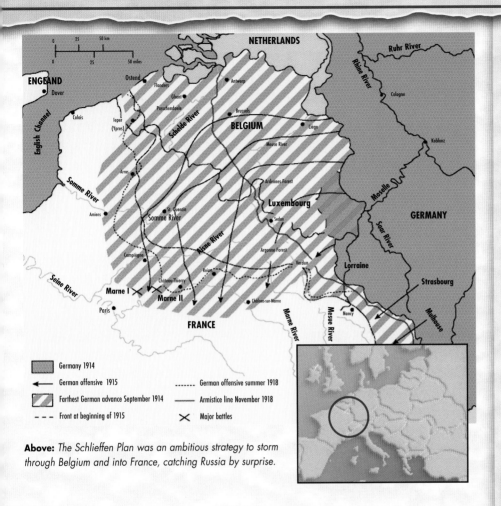

Above: *The Schlieffen Plan was an ambitious strategy to storm through Belgium and into France, catching Russia by surprise.*

Germany 1914
German offensive 1915
Farthest German advance September 1914
Front at beginning of 1915
German offensive summer 1918
Armistice line November 1918
Major battles

June 28, 1914
Archduke Ferdinand assassinated in Sarajevo, Bosnia.

July 29, 1914
Russia begins mobilization.

August 4, 1914
Britain declares war on Germany.

August 5–6, 1914
Belgian town of Hervé decimated by German troops in act of reprisal.

Below: *Helmuth von Moltke oversaw the Schlieffen Plan after Schlieffen died in 1913.*

Schlieffen died in 1913, so his successor, Helmuth von Moltke (1848–1916), was left to enact the plan. Moltke withdrew six western divisions and transferred them east, which fatally reduced the mass and momentum of the attack on France. The Battle of the Marne halted the German advance in September 1914. Today, arguments continue as to whether or not the Schlieffen Plan was workable from the start. In the meantime, nations across Europe built up their railroad lines and perfected their train schedules, all the while keeping in mind the idea of using the railroads as troop transport vehicles.

"He was worried about the Russian armaments, about the planned railway construction, and detected [in these] the preparations for a war against us in 1916. He complained about the inadequacy of the rail links that we had to the western front against France; and hinted . . . [at] whether or not it would not be better to strike now, rather than to wait."

In June 1914, banker Max Warburg recalled this conversation with Kaiser Wilhelm. The Kaiser was concerned about Germany's ability to move troops between the eastern and western fronts efficiently.

Above: *German troops amass outside Belgium in preparation for invasion.*

The German army invaded France, Belgium, and Luxembourg at the beginning of August 1914. This broke the terms of the 1839 Treaty of London, which guaranteed Belgium's neutrality. Britain entered the war on August 4, 1914. A preliminary British Expeditionary Force (BEF) of one hundred twenty thousand men began arriving in France on August 12, and quickly became involved in the Battle of Mons and the subsequent retreat. The German advance was rapid, efficient, and successful, pushing on toward Paris as Schlieffen had planned.

GERMANY ADVANCES TO THE GATES OF PARIS

Following the Schlieffen Plan, the German Fourth Army moved rapidly to occupy Luxembourg by August 3, and the Second Army crossed the Belgian border the following day. On August 16, after eleven days of German bombardment and siege, the fortified city of Liège, Belgium, capitulated. As Schlieffen had foreseen, the French, under General Joffre, responded by invading Alsace and Lorraine, far to the southeast of the exposed Belgian border. The French strike, Plan XVII, was a failure and drew valuable troops away from the area that the Germans planned to attack. On August 16, the German First Army, under Alexander von Kluck, invaded Belgium, took Brussels, then moved south. This action forced the French and the British Expeditionary Force (BEF), under Field Marshal Sir Douglas

"Happy are they who die, for they return Into the primeval clay and the primeval earth; Happy are they who die in a just war— Happy as the ripe corn and the harvested grain."

The early World War I recruits held romantic notions about the war. This paraphrased poem by French poet Charles Péguy illustrates how neither he nor anyone else understood what was to come. 🎵

"There was such a rush for fellows to go in the army that they'd had to get quite a number of officers in to deal with all these recruits . . . I was only eighteen and I didn't weigh very much—I didn't look very much like a soldier . . . but I was passed."

Gunner R. Lewis, Royal Garrison Artillery, recalls how he was admitted into the army.

Below: *General von Kluck (with overcoat) and his staff. He was an aggressive commander, a factor that contributed toward the failure of the Schlieffen Plan.*

Above: *French soldiers on the firing line at the First Battle of the Marne in France.*

TIME LINE

1914

August 3, 1914
German soldiers occupy Luxembourg.

August 13, 1914
German army invades Belgium.

August 24–30, 1914
British retreat from Mons, Belgium.

September 3, 1914
German cavalry patrols get within 8 miles (13 km) of Paris, France.

September 6–10, 1914
First battle of the Marne stops German advance and pushes them back east to the Chemin des Dames.

October 12 to November 11, 1914
First Battle of Ieper (Ypres)—neither side gains advantage.

Haig, to retreat from the Belgian cities of Charleroi and Mons. By early September, German forces had achieved a string of victories and were less than 30 miles (48 kilometers) from Paris, France.

THE BATTLE OF THE MARNE AND GERMAN RETREAT

The German advance had been spectacular, but its speed left exhausted soldiers in tattered uniforms who faced serious communication and logistical problems. Between September 5 and 10, French and British forces counter-attacked near Paris by the Marne River, in what has become known as the First Battle of the Marne. Armies attacked each other over open fields. Battle outcomes were mixed. French reinforcements arrived from Paris in taxis, and the French Fifth Army and the BEF advanced into the yawning gap

Left: *Countryside in the French region of Alsace, eastern France, was invaded during the Battle of the Marne.*

"In a side street off the Strand I met a jolly little dachshund—the dachshund might be called the national dog of Germany—walking cheerfully along well-bedecked in red, white, and blue ribbons. And around his neck he wore this label, 'I am a naturalised British subject.' And he seemed mighty proud of the fact, too."

On August 18, 1914, the Daily Mirror in England carried an article to illustrate to what bizarre extremes patriotism and anti-German feeling would go.

BRITONS
"WANTS YOU"
JOIN YOUR COUNTRY'S ARMY!
GOD SAVE THE KING
Reproduced by permission of LONDON OPINION

Left: *Lord Horatio Herbert Kitchener's famous 1914 poster aided recruitment into Britain's army.*

"The whole idea was to get hold of a rifle, learn to shoot a bit, proceed to France at the earliest possible moment, kill vast quantities of Germans, possibly get wounded in some artistic place, win the war and march back with Colours flying and bands playing and the girls falling on your neck."

Several million men responded to Lord Kitchener's call for volunteers in 1914 and 1915. They often joined up with a totally false idea of what was going to happen. Captain Alan Goring, M. C., recalls his expectations upon signing up.

between the German First and Second armies. By September 13, the Germans had retreated to the heights of the Chemin des Dames and east to Verdun. The Schlieffen Plan had failed.

THE CHRISTMAS TRUCES OF 1914

Unofficial and spontaneous Christmas truces took place at many sites along the western front during December 1914. Military authorities on both sides prohibited them, but German and British soldiers nevertheless met in no-man's-land, exchanged food and drink and chatted. At "Plug Street Wood" in Belgium, Captain C. I. Stockwell of the Royal Welch Fusiliers recalled how his truce ended at 8:30 A.M. On December 26, he fired three shots in

the air and put up a flag saying "Merry Christmas." The German captain responded by putting up a sheet with "Thank You" written on it. Both men climbed onto their parapets, bowed and saluted each other, and climbed back down into their trenches. The German captain fired two shots in the air and hostilities resumed.

A NEW KIND OF CONFLICT

By early 1915, it was clear that this was a new kind of war, a war of entrenched positions instead of rapid movement, and of large civilian armies rather than small professional ones. This type of mechanized, "total war" was a new phenomenon in history because it involved civilians as well as soldiers. Britain raised a huge volunteer army—Kitchener's

Right: *An artist's impression of the Christmas Truce in the Trenches, based on a description by a rifleman witness.*

LEST WE FORGET

The Sinking of the Lusitania.
May 7th 1915.

Above: *Poster commemorates the sinking of the luxury passenger ship the* Lusitania *by a German submarine.*

Army—and brought women into the munitions factories to free men to fight. The war created appalling conditions of combat and led to terrible wounds, the trauma of shell shock, and huge numbers of casualties. It also produced a new world of the trench and the dugout and produced enduring popular sayings, including "going over the top" (of a trench, into battle), and "no-man's-land"

What is **your** answer to Lord Kitchener's call?

"300,000 men wanted **now**."

Join an Irish Regiment
TO-DAY.

Is your conscience clear?

ENLIST TO-DAY

God Save the King

Above: *An advertisement in an Irish newspaper urges the male population to do the honorable thing and sign up.*

(the unoccupied area between armies) areas that we now call "demilitarized zones." The war also began to claim civilian casualties when, in May 1915, the German submarine *U-20* sank the unarmed passenger ship *Lusitania*. Nearly twelve hundred people drowned.

LEARNING THE HARD WAY

Nineteen fifteen was a bad year for the Allies. Flawed military tactics revealed the

TIME LINE
1914–1915

September 1914
After only six weeks of war, half a million British men volunteer for Kitchener's army.

September–October 1914
On the western front, German and Allied armies grind to a halt and trench warfare begins.

November 1915
Winston Churchill, First Lord of the Admiralty, suggests invading Turkey's Gallipoli peninsula.

December 1914
Unofficial Christmas truces between German and Allied soldiers occur at various places along the western front.

May 7, 1915
German submarine *U-20* sinks the passenger liner HMS *Lusitania* off the southern Irish coast.

"Enormous noise. Continuous explosion. A deserted landscape . . . Men were eating, smoking, doing odd jobs but no one was fighting. A few were peering in periscopes or looking through loopholes."

R. Mottram's first impressions of the front-line trenches. His bewildered reaction was typical of fresh recruits in WWI.

Above: *A Naval landing party coming into Kum Kaleh in Gallipoli, Turkey.*

> "One of the weapons contemplated was poison gas—in particular chlorine—which was blown towards the enemy from the most advanced positions. When I objected that this was a mode of warfare violating the Hague Convention, he said that the French had already started it . . ."

German officer Otto Hahn first heard in January 1915 that the Germans were to use poison gas on the battlefield around Ypres (Ieper), Belgium, in order to break the deadlock of the trenches.

Below: *A map showing the fateful Gallipoli invasion.*

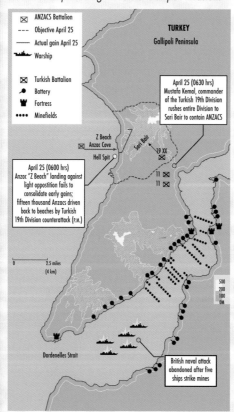

mismatch between nineteenth-century ideas and twentieth-century technology. On the battle line between the Allied and German armies, otherwise known as the western front, Allied forces won the battle of Neuve Chapelle in March, but suffered terrible losses in the Second Battle of Ypres (Ieper) in April and May, when the German attacked using poisonous gas. Between May 4 and June 18, the French suffered appalling casualties in the Second Battle of Artois, as did British and Indian troops at Aubers Ridge near Neuve Chapelle. After the Battle of Loos, France, from September 25 to October 16, almost 16,000 British were dead or missing and 34,580 wounded. No progress had been made. In an attempt to break the deadlock on the western front, the British government decided to open a new front, on the Gallipoli peninsula in Turkey.

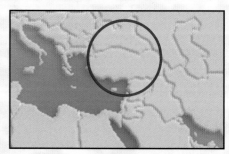

Above: *Australian troops survey the damage during the Gallipoli offensive of 1915.*

TIME LINE
1915–1916

March 10–13, 1915
Battle of Neuve Chapelle; Allies win control.

April 22–May 27, 1915
Second Battle of Ypres (Ieper), Belgium.

April 25, 1915
Allied troops land at Cape Helles on Turkey's Gallipoli peninsula.

December 1915– January 1916
Allied forces evacuate Gallipoli after two hundred thousand die.

GALLIPOLI 1915

Winston Churchill chose to attack Gallipoli, hoping to penetrate the Dardanelles strait and thus knock out Germany's ally, Turkey. Allied naval action failed, and several battleships were sunk by mines.

A mishandled land invasion on April 25 trapped British, French, and Anzac (Australian and New Zealand) troops on the beaches. The Turkish troops were commanded by German general Liman von Sanders. Mustapha Kemal, a Turk, distinguished himself in the battle. He later became Turkey's president under the name Kemal Atatürk. Allied attacks at Cape Helles, Anzac Cove, and Suvla Bay failed. Troops endured awful conditions and suffered appalling casualties. On October 16, Allied commander Sir Ian Hamilton was removed from power. Allied troops were evacuated in December. No advantage had been gained. Two hundred thousand Allied soldiers died.

Right: *Mustapha Kemal rose to prominence during the Gallipoli offensive against the Allies and later became president of Turkey.*

"We landed on a spit of land which in those days we called Shrapnel Point . . . There were lines of men clinging like cockroaches under the cliffs . . . The only thing to be done was to dig in . . . but a good many men were shot while they were doing this. . . . As it was, we had to put six hundred men on the ship from which we had embarked in the morning . . . under the charge of one officer, a veterinary surgeon!"

Landing on Gallipoli's beaches was a deadly situation, as recorded by
The Honorable Aubrey Herbert, a captain in the Irish Guards, on April 25, 1915.

Above: *Erich von Falkenhayn was criticized for his tactics at Verdun, France, that led to the deaths of tens of thousands of German soldiers.*

By the end of 1915, it was obvious to all sides that this was a war in which armies would attack each other from protective trenches. It was also clear that it would involve huge numbers of men and matériel. Ideas about how the war should be fought, however, did not keep pace with the new technologies of war. During 1916 and 1917, old ideas and new weapons came into conflict at the battles of Verdun, the Somme, and the Third Ypres (and nearby Passchendaele), leaving behind untold numbers of dead and wounded. These battles have become the icons of and bywords for the madness and futility of war.

"At my feet two unlucky creatures rolled the floor in misery. Their clothes and hands, their entire bodies were on fire. They were living torches. The next day: In front of us on the floor the two I had witnessed ablaze, lay rattling. They were so unrecognizably mutilated that we could not decide on their identities. Their skin was black entirely. One of them died that same night. In a fit of insanity, the other hummed a tune from his childhood, talked to his wife and his mother and spoke of his village. Tears were in our eyes."

French soldier Louis Barthas describes witnessing the horrific deaths of two German soldiers.

WHY VERDUN?

Verdun, ringed by protective forts along the Meuse River in northeast France, had no strategic value for either the Germans or the French. Nevertheless, it became the bloodiest battleground of the war, with about 715,000 casualties. In February 1916, prompted by his policy of attrition, German General Erich von Falkenhayn chose to attack Verdun. He aimed not for a breakthrough, but rather to wear down the French army. French commander General Joseph Joffre was so confident that the forts of Douaumont, Vaux, and Thiaumont could withstand attack that just before the battle he had their defenses dismantled and their guns removed.

SACRED BATTLEFIELD

On February 21, 1916, the Germans bombarded the French lines with a million shells, and within a few days Fort Douaumont fell. Joffre was immediately replaced by General Pétain, commander of the French Second Army. From this point, Verdun became a symbol of France's will to endure and win, and the prospect of defeat or surrender was considered a political impossibility. Falkenhayn's hope that his attack would suck in virtually the entire French army was realized when 259 of the 330 French infantry

Below: *French troops prepare for battle at Fort Douaumont at Verdun.*

Above: *Paul von Hindenburg (left) with Kaiser Wilhelm and Erich von Ludendorff, planning battle lines.*

TIME LINE
1916

February 21, 1916
Germans launch artillery barrage and attack on Verdun.

February 22–29, 1916
Fierce fighting and German capture of Fort Douaumont.

April 20, 1916
French counterattack repulsed by the German army.

divisions became embroiled in the carnage. A series of attacks and counterattacks raged from February to November, with gas, artillery, airplanes, and flamethrowers all used in the desperate struggle. Fort Vaux was overrun by the Germans in June. The French retook Fort Douaumont in October. No side could win a decisive advantage, and the battle became a deadly grinding machine for both armies. As Christmas approached, it became clear that the French had held on and Verdun was saved.

Below: *Rows of crosses mark the graves of soldiers killed at Verdun, France.*

BATTLE OF THE SOMME

The Somme offensive was originally planned for December 1915 as a joint British and French attack designed to wear down the German army's reserve forces. The German attack on Verdun in February 1916 changed things dramatically. French soldiers were drawn away from the

"The losses are registered as follows: They are dead, wounded, missing, nervous wrecks, ill, and exhausted. Nearly all suffer from dysentery. Because of the failing provisioning, the men are forced to use up their emergency rations of salty meats. They quenched their thirst with water from the shellholes. They have to build their own accommodation and are given a little cacao to stop the diarrhea. The latrines, wooden beams hanging over open holes, are occupied day and night—the holes are filled with slime and blood."

A German witness writes about the state of his fellow soldiers during the Verdun offensive in 1916.

Above: *Allied soldiers taking part in trench warfare during the Battle of the Somme.*

Somme to reinforce Verdun, leaving the bulk of the attack to the British Fourth Army, commanded by Sir Henry Rawlinson. The disastrous outcome was partly due to the fact that there were two different battle plans.

Rawlinson favored a "bite-and-hold" operation involving heavy artillery bombardment, followed by the infantry seizing and defending parts of the German lines before repeating. Haig, the commander of the British Expeditionary Forces (BEF), favored an infantry breakthrough followed by a lightning cavalry advance. As a result, the offensive that finally started in July coupled an intense artillery barrage with heavy infantry attacks in the northern and central sectors.

"July 10, 1916. Dawn patrol. This is the most impressive time of day to be out. The light has barely come and gun flashes twinkle all over the country in little points of blue flame. From time to time, rockets soar up into the grey dawn. Flares glow like fires in the trenches and far over in Hun-land the white plume of a train."

Logbook entry by Cecil Lewis, a pilot in the Royal Flying Corps (RFC) regarding the Battle of the Somme.

Right: *The Battle of the Somme, 1916.*

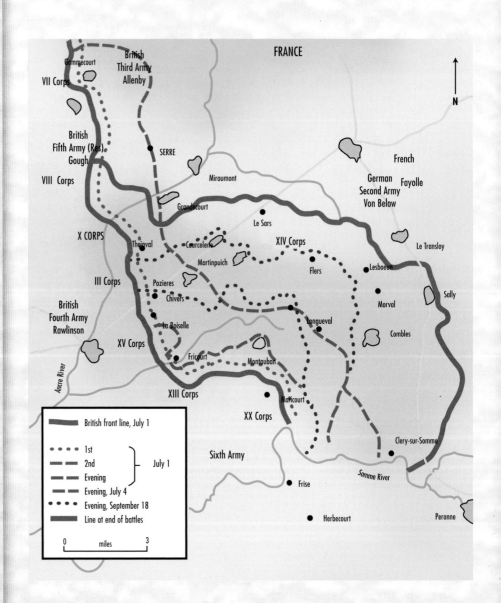

FRANCE

Gommecourt
British Third Army Allenby
VII Corps
SERRE
British Fifth Army (Res.) Gough
VIII Corps
Miraumont
Grandcourt
French
German Second Army Von Below
Fayolle
Le Sars
X CORPS
Thiepval
Courcelette
Martinpuich
XIV Corps
Le Transloy
Flers
Lesboeufs
III Corps
Pozieres
Chivers
Sally
British Fourth Army Rawlinson
La Boiselle
Morval
Longueval
Combles
XV Corps
Fricourt
Montauban
Ancre River
XIII Corps
Maricourt
XX Corps
Clery-sur-Somme
Sixth Army
Frise
Somme River
Peronne
Herbecourt

N

Legend:
- British front line, July 1
- · · · · 1st
- – – – 2nd (July 1)
- ▬ ▬ Evening (July 1)
- ▬ ▬ Evening, July 4
- • • • Evening, September 18
- Line at end of battles

0 — miles — 3

DECISIVE BATTLES

British soldiers subjected the German positions to five days of bombardment, then went "over the top" in the early hours of July 1, 1916. Weighed down with equipment, soldiers advanced in a line at a walking pace to disastrous results. German machine gunners slaughtered the advancing British. By nightfall, twenty thousand men were dead and forty thousand were wounded—the worst day in the British army's history. Despite the mistakes, the battle continued for another six months following similar tactics. By its end, Allied casualties at the Somme rose to more than six hundred thousand. German casualties reached nearly four hundred fifty thousand.

Above: *King George V (center) with, (left to right), Marshal Joffre, General Poincare, General Foch, and Field Marshal Haig at Beauquesne, France.*

YPRES: SIX BATTLES IN ONE

Historians still fiercely debate Haig's strategy for ordering the attacks on the strong German defenses at Ypres about one year after the beginning of the Somme offensive. The Third Battle of Ypres began on July 31, 1917. Its immediate objective was to capture a strategic ridge named for the small town, Passchendaele, on the ridge. Allied troops advanced over terrain churned up by artillery fire and turned into mud by rain. The

TIME LINE
1916

June 24, 1916
Allied artillery bombardment of German lines begins during Battle of Somme.

July 1, 1916
British and French troops go "over the top" to the German trenches.

July 2–10, 1916
British fail to break through in the center, but French have some success on the right wing.

July 12 to August 27, 1916
Allied attacks and German counterattacks.

September 15–22, 1916
Battle of Flers-Courcellete; no significant Allied gains.

September 25 to November 19, 1916
Battle of the Ancre; Allies fail to break through German lines.

Above: *Soldiers load wounded comrades into an ambulance at Verdun.*

> "That was a stupid action, because we had to make a frontal attack on bristling German guns and there was no shelter at all . . . There were dead bodies all over the place . . . We just couldn't take High Wood against machine guns. It was just absolute slaughter."

Sergeant Bill Hay, 9th Battalion, Royal Scots, 51st Division, recalls an attack on "High Wood," one of many fruitless and bloody attacks during the six months of the Somme battle in France.

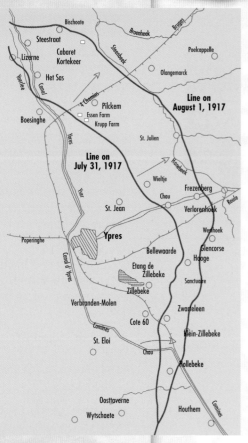

Third Battle of Ypres was, in fact, six separate battles: the Battle of the Menin Road; the Battle of Polygon Wood; the Battle of Broodseinde; the Battle of Poelkapelle, and the First and Second battles of Passchendaele. Continued attacks against German defenses failed. Allied forces finally won on the Menin Road, at Polygon Wood, and at Broodseinde, and on November 5, 1917, Canadian troops captured Passchendaele itself. Four months of fighting and five hundred thousand casualties brought no obvious Allied gain. During three days in April 1918, the Germans recaptured Passchendaele ridge.

UNITED STATES ENTERS WAR

In early 1917, meanwhile, Germany announced that its U-boats had adopted a new policy of unrestricted warfare in the Atlantic. What really turned U.S. public opinion toward favoring the war was the interception of a secret message between Germany and Mexico. Germany promised to hand over Texas, New Mexico, and Arizona to Mexico in return for joining the German side of the war. After U-boats

Left and above: *Map showing the advance of troops toward Passchendaele during the Third Battle of Ypres in Belgium.*

Right: *Lord Haig was a controversial military leader whose tactics led to terrible casualties among his own troops.*

"The conditions are awful, beyond description . . . a desolate wilderness of water filled with shell craters . . . Here a shattered wagon, there a gun mired to the muzzle in mud which grips like glue, even the birds and rats have forsaken so unnatural a spot. Mile after mile of the same unending dreariness, landmarks are gone, of whole villages hardly a pile of bricks amongst the mud marks the site. You see it best under a leaden sky with a chill drizzle falling, each hour an eternity, each dragging step a nightmare. How weirdly it recalls some half formed horror of childish nightmare. . . Surely the God of Battles has deserted a spot where only devils can reign."

Major John Lyne of the 64th Brigade, Royal Field Artillery, observed the appalling conditions during the Third Battle of Ypres in 1917. The town of Passchendaele was devastated by the mortar attacks that went on around it.

sunk three American shipping vessels in three days that March, President Wilson convinced Congress to declare war on Germany in April 1917. Other Western Hemisphere countries, especially in the Caribbean, soon followed suit. The U.S. Navy responded almost immediately, while it took the U.S. Army longer to train and equip its troops. U.S. soldiers finally landed in France in June 1917, but the American forces didn't reach full strength until about March 1918. The full impact of the U.S. "Doughboys," commanded by General John Pershing, broke through German lines in September 1918. After some stalling, the message was soon clear: Germany would lose this war.

Above: *Soldiers advance through Chateau Wood during the Third Battle of Ypres.*

TIME LINE
1917

April 6, 1917
U.S. declares war on Germany.

June 1917
U.S. troops land in France.

July 16, 1917
British bombardment of Passchendaele, Belgium.

September 20–25, 1917
Battle of the Menin Road.

July 31– November 5, 1917
Third Battle of Ypres at Passchendaele.

Left: *Ordered rows of graves fill Tynecot Cemetery at Passchendaele, Belgium.*

"The bombardment was murderous—ours and the Germans'—and they weren't only flinging over shells, they were simply belting machine-gun fire for all they were worth . . . The shells were falling thick and fast and by some sort of capillary action the holes they made filled with water as you looked at them."

Private J. Pickard, 7th Winnipeg Grenadiers, recalls the final push for Passchendaele.

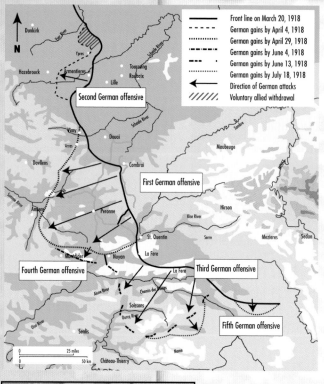

Front line on March 20, 1918
German gains by April 4, 1918
German gains by April 29, 1918
German gains by June 4, 1918
German gains by June 13, 1918
German gains by July 18, 1918
Direction of German attacks
Voluntary allied withdrawal

Left and above: *Map of the failed German offensives that began in the spring of 1918.*

After four years of bitter conflict, the Great War came to an end on November 11, 1918. It left in its wake millions of shattered lives. Over all, seventy million men had been mobilized, more than ten million had died, and millions more suffered wounds. Millions of widows and fatherless children were also left behind. The shape of Europe changed forever: The monarchies of Germany, Austro-Hungary, and Russia were deposed and the United States stood on the brink of becoming a major world power. Reparations and war guilt were heaped on Germany, laying the foundations for a second conflict that would eventually give the Great War its alternative name: World War I.

ARMISTICE AT THE ELEVENTH HOUR

The failure of the German offensive and the ensuing success of the Allied advance beyond the Hindenburg Line in northern France caused a collapse of morale in the German army. Although German lines were not breached, on October 3, 1918, German prince Max von Baden wrote to President Woodrow Wilson asking for a U.S.-brokered armistice. Exactly one month later, Austro-Hungary surrendered, and on October 30, Turkey followed. On November 6, in a railroad car at Compiègne, Germany signed an armistice that would take effect at 11 A.M. on November 11, 1918. Germany agreed to withdraw from all occupied territories on the western and eastern fronts and to surrender its navy. On December 1, the Allies began their occupation of the Rhineland, the part of western Germany that allowed for strategic control of the rest of the country. The "war to end all wars" was over.

"We have no jealousy of German greatness, and there is nothing in this program that impairs it. We grudge her no achievement or distinction of learning or of pacific enterprise such as have made her record very bright and very enviable. We do not wish to injure her or to block in any way her legitimate influence or power."

U.S. president Woodrow Wilson summed up the sentiments behind U.S. war goals in a speech to Congress on January 8, 1918. He outlined what became known as his "Fourteen Points."

CELEBRATIONS AND REFLECTIONS

Victorious nations celebrated the signing of the Armistice. London, England, filled with crowds of singing and cheering soldiers and civilians, and people embraced each other. In Paris, France, crowds sang themselves hoarse with endless renditions of the French national anthem, "La Marseillaise." Newspapers and placards announced: "The Armistice is signed," and patriotic crowds dragged captured German artillery around the streets. Crowds in Sydney, Australia, cheered as an effigy of the Kaiser was first hanged, then burned. By contrast, Armistice Day in Germany was a sad affair. Some wept openly. The war was lost, the Kaiser had abdicated, the authoritarian Wilhelmine government was gone. Germany's future looked grim.

THE TREATY OF VERSAILLES

On June 28, 1919, the leaders of the Allied forces gathered in the Hall of Mirrors at the Palace of Versailles near Paris to work out the terms of the peace settlement. The defeated German government could not dispute the proposed terms. Under the treaty, Germany had to accept responsibility for

Above: *German prince Max von Baden negotiated an armistice with the Allies.*

Below: *On Armistice Day, the Perkins Building in Tacoma, Washington, displayed a seven-story flag.*

TIME LINE
1918

October 3, 1918
Germany asks U.S. president Wilson to broker peace.

November 6, 1918
Germany signs the Armistice.

November 11, 1918
10:58 a.m. Canadian private George Price becomes one of the war's last casualties.

November 11, 1918
11 A.M.—Armistice takes effect.

June 28, 1919
Treaty of Versailles ends war.

November 15, 1920
First League of Nations meeting.

Above: *A selection of medals awarded to British servicemen for fighting in World War I.*

"The Kaiser and King has decided to renounce the throne. The Imperial Chancellor will remain in office until the questions connected with the abdication of the Kaiser, the renouncing by the Crown Prince of the throne of the German Empire and of Prussia, and the setting up of a regency have been settled. For the regency, he intends to appoint Deputy Ebert as Imperial Chancellor, and he proposes that a bill shall be brought in for the establishment of a law providing for the immediate promulgation of general suffrage and for a constitutional German National Assembly, which will settle finally the future form of government of the German Nation and of those peoples which might be desirous of coming within the empire."

Prince Max von Baden's announcement of Kaiser Wilhelm II's abdication on November 9, 1918.

Below and right: *Map of Germany's losses following the Treaty of Versailles.*

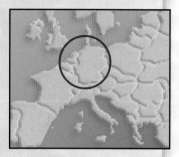

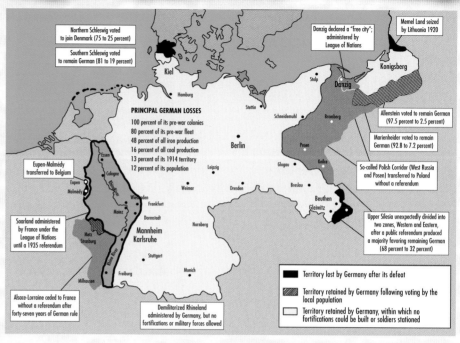

Northern Schleswig voted to join Denmark (75 to 25 percent)

Southern Schleswig voted to remain German (81 to 19 percent)

Danzig declared a "free city"; administered by League of Nations

Memel Land seized by Lithuania 1920

Konigsberg

Kiel

Stolp

Danzig

Hamburg

Stettin

Schneidemuhl

Bromberg

Allenstein voted to remain German (97.5 percent to 2.5 percent)

PRINCIPAL GERMAN LOSSES

100 percent of its pre-war colonies
80 percent of its pre-war fleet
48 percent of all iron production
16 percent of all coal production
13 percent of its 1914 territory
12 percent of its population

Berlin

Posen

Glogau

Kalice

Marienheider voted to remain German (92.8 to 7.2 percent)

So-called Polish Corridor (West Russia and Posen) transferred to Poland without a referendum

Eupen-Malmédy transferred to Belgium

Essen

Cologne

Leipzig

Weimar

Dresden

Breslau

Beuthen

Gleiwitz

Eupen

Malmedy

Wiesbaden

Frankfurt

Mainz

Darmstadt

Saarland administered by France under the League of Nations until a 1935 referendum

Metz
Strasburg

Mannheim
Karlsruhe

Nurnberg

Upper Silesia unexpectedly divided into two zones, Western and Eastern, after a public referendum produced a majority favoring remaining German (68 percent to 32 percent)

Stuttgart

Munich

Territory lost by Germany after its defeat

Territory retained by Germany following voting by the local population

Territory retained by Germany, within which no fortifications could be built or soldiers stationed

Milhausen

Freiburg

Alsace-Lorraine ceded to France without a referendum after forty-seven years of German rule

Demilitarized Rhineland administered by Germany, but no fortifications or military forces allowed

On November 11, 1920, at the unveiling of the Cenotaph in London, a *Daily Herald* special Correspondent wrote:

"When the first stroke of Big Ben sounded over Whitehall, the king, standing in the middle of the road, surrounded by admirals and field marshals, turned southwards to face the *Cenotaph*.

"On the last stroke of eleven, the king pressed a knob on the top of a little pedestal erected in the road, and two great Union Jacks that draped the Cenotaph fell to the ground. At the same moment, the king raised his cap. Bareheaded and silent, he stood in the midst of this vast gathering of the silent people."

starting the war. It also had to promise to pay reparations (compensation) of more than $1.6 million (in 1919 dollars) for the damage it had caused. Its army and navy were severely restricted. The German navy was cut to just six battleships. The army had to drop down to one hundred thousand soldiers. German territory in Europe was confiscated and it lost its African colonies. Finally, the treaty prevented Germany from uniting with Austria or joining the League of Nations.

REMEMBERING THE WAR

After the war, the world took stock of the conflict's terrible consequences. In Europe, Britain and France put a huge effort into commemorating the sacrifices made by their people. On November 11, 1920, the Cenotaph in London was unveiled in the presence of the king, and the coffin of the unknown soldier, a single corpse that represented thousands, was laid to rest in Westminster Abbey. The first of many two-minute silences was

"He is not missing: He is here! No words can express our feelings adequately but they will be expressed for us by the familiar bugle calls which we shall hear on the conclusion of the service."

On July 24, 1927, the Menin Gate Memorial to the Missing at Ypres, Belgium, was inaugurated. On it are engraved the names of fifty-five thousand soldiers whose bodies have never been identified. Field Marshal Herbert Plumer addressed the crowds and began the tradition of a bugler playing "The Last Post," a song similar to the American "Taps." It is still played every day.

🎞 **FILM EXCERPT** 📖 **GOVERNMENT DOCUMENT** 🎙 **INTERVIEW/BOOK EXTRACT** 🎵 **SONG EXCERPT/POEM**

Right: *Thiepval, a memorial on an isolated, windswept area near the Somme River, commemorates British and French soldiers. Its walls hold the names of more than seventy-three thousand Somme veterans.*

observed. Across the country in the years that followed local war memorials were erected, as were memorial libraries and hospitals. On July 24, 1927, the Menin Gate Memorial in Ypres, Belgium, was inaugurated in memory of fifty-five thousand soldiers with no known grave. On July 31, 1932, the Thiepval Memorial to the more than seventy-three thousand soldiers missing on the Somme battlefields was unveiled.

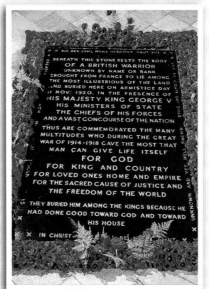

TIME LINE
1919–1920

1919–1939
Battlefield pilgrimages at their height.

1919
Paul Nash paints *The Menin Road.*

November 11, 1920
London: The Cenotaph unveiled; unknown soldier buried in Westminster Abbey.

Left: *Flowers decorate the grave of the unknown soldier in London, England.*

Bottom: *(left to right, front) British prime minister Lloyd George, French premier Georges Clemenceau, and U.S. president Woodrow Wilson walk together in Paris during negotiations for the Treaty of Versailles.*

The Unknown Soldier

"Great silent crowds watched yesterday's supremely impressive tribute paid to an unknown 'common soldier.' The unveiling of the Cenotaph in Whitehall by the king, the procession thence to Westminster, and the service in the great national Abbey were of deep significance, but most impressive of all was the two minutes of universal silence."

Daily Herald special correspondent, at the official unveiling of the tomb of the unknown soldier in Westminster Abbey, London, England, November 12, 1920.

I n art, literature, film, and photography, four years of conflict redefined the ways in which people saw themselves, each other, and their relationships with technology. The influences of war and its aftermath saturated popular culture. New ways of seeing the world led to avant-garde art such as Cubism and new fashions such as Art Deco. Poetry, fiction, and other writing became less romanticized and more realistic. Advances in film and camera technology helped launch the Hollywood era.

Above: *German artist Otto Dix painted* Der Schützengraben (The Trench) *between 1920 and 1923.*

PAINTING THE WAR

The Great War produced a dramatic shift in art. Painters found they could no longer express their experiences in pre-1914 ways and developed new and unconventional styles. In Britain, artists such as C. R. W. Nevinson, Wyndham Lewis, and Paul Nash typified this new approach. In 1919, Nash's *The Menin Road* captured the spirit of war's devastation of the landscape. French artists produced a mix of old and new in the famous style of *images d'epinal*. These placed the current war in a grander context of French history. The 1915 drawing *The End of the War* by Raoul Dufy is a collage that includes the Gallic symbol of a young rooster, Joan of Arc, General Joffre, and Rheims cathedral aflame after German bombardment. In Germany, Otto Dix portrayed the grotesque nature of his war

During the filming of ***All Quiet on the Western Front***, so many (and often bizarre) cuts were made by the censors of different countries that the original uncut film has never been seen; In June 1930, for example, the film was released in Canada with the following deletions:

dialogue in reel 3: "When you come back you'll all get some nice clean underwear."
Close-up of boy in hysterics in reel 4

Eliminate words "in the backside" from line ...
"I ought to give you a kick in the backside"

Below: *The Menin Road by Paul Nash. As a commissioned officer, Nash produced hundreds of detailed sketches of life in the trenches on the western front that he later developed into paintings.*

experiences. His famous painting *Flanders* mixes the nightmarish imagery of Hieronymus Bosch with the effects of industrialized war on human beings.

PHOTOGRAPHY AND FILM

Photography and film also underwent dramatic developments during and after the war. Official war photographers took pictures for propaganda, aerial photography was perfected for planning battles, and individuals took their own personal photos. Three kinds of movies were made: newsreels of actual events, government-approved war films such as *The Somme* (1927), and Hollywood productions that

Above *A poster advertises the 1969 movie, "Oh! What a Lovely War," directed by Richard Attenborough.*

presented the war in epic terms, spiced with romance and heroism. *Wings* (1927), *Hell's Angels* (1930), *Westfront* (1931) and *A Farewell to Arms* (1932) all portrayed stunning but ambiguous views of the war. Decades later, films such as Stanley Kubrick's *Paths to Glory* (1957) and Richard Attenborough's *Oh! What a Lovely War* (1969) continued to explore contentious issues raised by the Great War.

Left: *Silent film star Clara Bow starred in the movie* Wings *in 1927.*

"I have seen the most frightful nightmare of a country more conceived by Dante . . . than by nature, unspeakable, utterly indescribable. In the fifteen drawings I have made I may give you some idea of its horror . . . We all have a vague notin of the terrors of a battle . . . but no pen or drawing can convey this . . . Evil and the incarnate fiend alone can be master of this war and no glimmer of God's hand is seen anywhere. Sunset and sunrise are blasphemous, they are mockeries to man, only the black rain . . . is fit atmosphere in such a land."

Shaken by his experiences in the Ypres salient, artist Paul Nash wrote to his wife, Margaret, in November 1917.

TIME LINE
1927–1931

JULY 24, 1927
Unveiling of the Menin Gate memorial to the missing in Ypres, Belgium.

1928
Publication of *Undertones of War*, by Edmund Blunden; *Memoirs of a Fox-Hunting Man*, by Siegfried Sassoon.

1929
Publication of *Good-Bye to All That*, by Robert Graves; *The Storm of Steel*, by Ernst Jünger; *All Quiet on the Western Front*, by Erich Maria Remarque.

1930
Release of the films *All Quiet on the Western Front*, *Westfront*, and *Hell's Angels*. Publication of *Memoirs of an Infantry Officer*, by Siegfried Sasson.

Above: *A cover from the popular British publication,* The Illustrated War News.

NEWSPAPERS, MAGAZINES, AND POSTERS

In a world before television or radio, news of the war came mainly from the printed media—newspapers, magazines, and posters. Propaganda fueled much of this coverage, and government censors deleted anything regarded as too militarily sensitive or likely to reduce patriotic support for the war. Most wartime magazines were heavily illustrated with photographs and artist's impressions that sanitized military disasters and downplayed casualties. In Britain, *The Illustrated War News*, in France *Le Miroir* and *L'Illustration*, and in Germany the *Illustrierte Zeitung* all tailored their images and stories to suit their government's restrictions. In the battle zones, soldiers produced their own trench newspapers such as the *British Wipers Times*, whose name was soldier's slang for "Ypres."

WAR POETRY AND MEMOIRS

In wartime poetry and postwar memoirs written in English, a new language emerged to express the human experiences of war. Although written mainly by educated middle-class soldiers, poems by Wilfred Owen, Ivor Gurney, and Isaac Rosenberg captured the futility of war and the immensity of its tragedy. A decade after 1918, many classic memoirs began to appear, often

Right *War poet Robert Graves.*

"One by one, my contemporaries were sent out to France to take the place of casualties in the First and Second Battalions, while I remained despondently at the depôt.

"At Béthune, I saw the ghost of a man named Private Challoner, who had been at Lancaster with me . . . [he] looked in at the window, saluted, and passed on. I jumped up, looked out of the window, and saw nothing except a fag-end smoking on the pavement. Challoner had been killed at Festubert in May."

Good-Bye to All That, **by British author Robert Graves, was published in 1931 and again in 1957 with revisions. It is among the most famous British Great War memoirs.**

written by authors already known for writing poetry. Siegfried Sassoon published his trilogy of autobiographical war novels—*Memoirs of a Fox-Hunting Man*, *Memoirs of an Infantry Officer*, and *Sherston's Progress*. Robert Graves wrote *Good-Bye to All That*, and Edmund Blunden published *Undertones of War*. War poems and memoirs fixed the memory of the war in the public consciousness. Many of these works remain powerful reminders of the futility of war.

Above: *In Germany, the* Illustrierte Zeitung, *a news magazine, portrayed the war from a more positive perspective.*

TRENCH ART

The study of trench art is an important feature of the new archaeological interest in the Great War. Trench art describes objects made by soldiers, prisoners of war, and civilians during and after the war as souvenirs and mementos. The most common form of trench art was created from recycled war matériel such as metal scrap and bullets, sometimes decorated with regimental badges and personalized inscriptions. The most popular pieces were decorated artillery shell cases. These objects are found in museums and in people's homes as well as in excavations, and illustrate the human dimension of war.

TIME LINE
1932

JULY 31, 1932
The Memorial to the Missing at Thiepval on the Somme is unveiled.

1932
Release of the movie, *A Farewell to Arms*, from the book by Ernest Hemingway.

Above: *British war poet Wilfred Owen.*

"Gas! Gas! Quick, boys—an ecstasy
  of fumbling,
Fitting the clumsy helmets just in time,
But someone still was yelling out
  and stumbling
And floundering like a man in fire or lime . . .

. . . If you could hear, at every jolt,
The blood come gargling from the froth-corrupted lungs,
Obscene as cancer, bitter as the cud
Of vile incurable sores on innocent tongues,
My friend, you would not tell with such high zest
To children ardent for desperate glory,
The old lie: 'Dulce et Decorum est pro patria mori.'"

Extract from"Dulce et Decorum Est," (It is sweet and right to die for your country) one of Wilfred Owen's most famous and often-quoted poems.

Above: *When Germany could not pay its reparations, French and Belgian troops occupied the Ruhr, the center of Germany's coal, iron, and steel production.*

The Great War and its aftermath changed forever the political and economic shape of the world. It created the powerhouse of the United States, demolished imperial Europe, created new nations, fostered bitter and still-lingering ethnic tensions, and moved the world relentlessly toward World War II. Since the 1960s, Europe has experienced a surge of interest in WWI that has spawned tourism to the western front battlefields, museums, and memorials.

Below: *Dictator Adolf Hitler rose to power during the collapse of the German economy.*

TOWARD A NEW WAR

World War I officially ended with the Treaty of Versailles on June 28, 1919. As many leaders foresaw at the time, the terms were so harsh for Germany that they bred only resentment and political extremism.

The "war to end all wars" became instead a twenty-year-long prelude to the outbreak of World War II in 1939. The aftermath of the Versailles Treaty during the interwar years changed the shape of the world.

Despite the fact that the Versailles Treaty had embodied some of President Woodrow Wilson's Fourteen Points for World Peace, the United States Senate refused to ratify the Treaty of Versailles. Precisely when American leadership was required, the U.S. slid further into an isolationist policy. This precluded any help with global financial restructuring and debt repayment. Many Germans believed that their army had not been defeated, and that incompetent politicians and communist agitators had caused a collapse from within. German humiliation amplified when French troops occupied the German

"The treaty includes no provisions for the economic rehabilitation of Europe—nothing to make the defeated Central empires into good neighbors, nothing to stabilize the new states of Europe, nothing to reclaim Russia; nor does it promote in any way a compact of economic solidarity amongst the Allies themselves; no arrangement was reached at Paris for restoring the disordered finances of France and Italy or to adjust the systems of the Old World and the New."

From The Economic Consequences of the Peace by John Maynard Keynes.

industrial region of the Ruhr in 1921 when Germany defaulted on repayment. Restrictions imposed on the size of the German army by the Versailles Treaty caused many German ex-soldiers to join far-right extremist groups during the social and economic chaos of the 1920s. These factors, combined with the German government's inability to deal with the rampant inflation, culminated in the formation of the National Socialist German Workers' Party (the Nazi Party). Adolf Hitler, who was appointed chancellor of Germany in 1933, led the Nazis.

A NEW EUROPE

In the rest of Europe, also, the interwar period saw ominous political developments. Italians felt they had been poorly treated at Versailles despite being on the Allied side. This gave Benito Mussolini and his followers, the *Fascisti*, or Fascists, the opportunity to seize political power in Italy. The political map of eastern Europe changed also. Finland, Poland, Czechoslovakia, and Yugoslavia formed after 1919. These new countries had weak governments that did little other than create a bitterly divisive legacy for the future. This legacy continued into World War II, and lasted through the Cold War and the collapse of the Soviet empire during the 1980s. It eventually contributed to the bitter struggles in Bosnia-Herzegovina and Kosovo during the 1990s.

Above: *Fascist dictator Benito Mussolini rose to power in Italy during the national unrest caused by the harsh terms established by the Treaty of Versailles.*

TIME LINE
1939–1964

1939–1964
Interest in World War I ebbs.

1964
In Britain, the broadcast of the BBC's *The Great War* stimulates renewed interest in World War I.

In Europe, battlefield tourism to the western front becomes popular.

Below: *Despite President Woodrow Wilson's role in formulating the Treaty of Versailles, the United States became more isolationistic after World War I.*

"National aspirations must be respected; people may now be dominated and governed only by their own consent. 'Self determination' is not a mere phrase. It is an imperative principle of action, which statesmen will henceforth ignore at their peril. This war had its roots in the disregard of the rights of small nations and of nationalities which lacked the union and the force to make good their claim to determine their own allegiances and their own forms of political life. Covenants must now be entered into which will render such things impossible for the future; and those covenants must be backed by the united force of all nations that love justice and are willing to maintain it at any cost . . . "

Excerpt from speech to U.S. Congress by President Woodrow Wilson, February 11, 1919.

Above: *Four U.S. representatives arrive at the conference at Lausannes, Switzerland, in 1922 to decide the future of the Ottoman Empire. From left to right are Mr. Berlin, Secretary-General; Ambassador Child, U.S. representative at Rome, Italy; Mr. Lorio, U.S. Minister at Bern, Switzerland; and Mr. Armory, Secretary of the U.S. delegation.*

"Dear James,

Whilst perhaps enjoyment is the wrong word to use we did enjoy your excellent guiding. We are both glad we went and somehow
I feel it was something that as many people as possible should try and do in order to understand better the horrors of War. I will never forget the emotion of standing under the Thiepval Memorial and trying to comprehend the massive scale
of killing that took place and what little was achieved, but I suppose we can all claim the knowledge of hindsight."

A letter of thanks written to Somme Battlefield Tours Limited, a European company that offers guided tours of World War I battlefields.

PROBLEMS IN THE MIDDLE EAST

The Middle East also suffered the consequences of the Versailles Treaty in ways that created profound tensions throughout the region for many decades. Arab lands freed when Germany's ally, the Ottoman Empire, surrendered were not granted independence at Versailles. Large areas of Middle Eastern land was arbitrarily divided. Territorial boundaries were redrawn. Britain and France often served in the position of overseeing these new nations. Such political situations sowed the seeds of many current Middle Eastern problems associated with nationalism, religion, and the control of oil production.

BATTLEFIELD TOURISM

During the interwar years, tens of thousands visited the battlefields of the western front. Clutching old letters, maps, and guidebooks, they journeyed to the Somme and Ypres, stopping briefly at the sites and towns associated with four years of war. They stayed in local hotels, ate and drank in cafés and bars, and bought battlefield souvenirs to take home. Battlefield tourism helped rebuild shattered local economies. World War II (WWII) brought battlefield pilgrimages of WWI sites to an abrupt end. After WWII ended, television helped restimulate the desire for tours of western front battlefields, especially among Europeans. During the early 1970s, about fifty thousand visitors a year traveled to WWI battlefields.
By 1974, this had grown to roughly one quarter of a million tourists. Inquiries to Britain's Commonwealth War Graves Commission (CWGC) regarding the whereabouts of WWI graves rose from about fifteen hundred a year in the mid-1960s to twenty-eight thousand annually in 1990. Those numbers continue to grow. Increasing numbers of battlefield tour companies, hotels, and cafés, cater to tourists. The Ypres, Belgium, "Last Post" ceremony that occurs

Left: *Battlefield tourists view a reconstructed trench in the Somme.*

Above: *Bugles play during the "Last Post" ceremony at Ypres, Belgium.*

TIME LINE
1990–1998

1990
Digging begins, mainly by local amateur groups; professional excavations in France begin. Battlefield reclamation and scavenging occurs.

1992
The *Historial de la Grande Guerre* opens in Peronne near the Somme in France.

1997
Professional excavations begin at Auchonvillers on the Somme; investigations of trench art begin.

1998
The *In Flanders Fields* Museum opens in Ypres, Belgium.

every evening at 8 P.M. attracts large numbers of visitors.

MUSEUMS, MONUMENTS, AND HERITAGE

Renewed interest in WWI tourism began gaining momentum in the 1960s. By the 1990s, interest in WWI changed into an iconic cultural event, evolving into a potent mix of tourism that includes visits to battlefields, war cemeteries, museums, and exhibitions. The idea of war as heritage has arrived. In Britain, a National Inventory of War Memorials now exists, and the Imperial War Museum organizes major exhibitions. Increasing numbers of young and old observe the two-minute silence on November 11. In France and Belgium, the "Western Front Experience" has become very popular. Tourist boards in Ypres and on the Somme organize special events, and local hotels, restaurants, and shops associate themselves with Great War imagery.

Below: *A dramatic view of the Imperial War Museum in London, England.*

"The United States Congress created the Veterans History Project in 2000. It collects oral history interviews, memoirs, letters, diaries, photographs, and other original materials from veterans of World Wars I and II, and the Korean, Vietnam, and Persian Gulf Wars and the Afghanistan and Iraq conflicts (2001–present). Those U.S. citizen civilians who were actively involved in supporting war efforts (such as war industry workers, USO workers, flight instructors, medical volunteers, etc.) are also encouraged to contribute their personal narratives. Members of the public become part of the Veterans History Project after they donate their materials."

From the U.S. Library of Congress Veterans History Project.

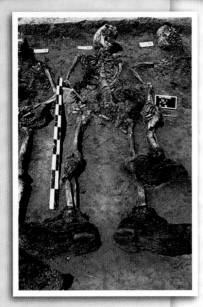

Above: *In 2001, archeaologists in the city of Arras in northern France discovered the remains of twenty-four British WWI soldiers who were buried in 1917. They were unearthed during the excavations for a new BMW car factory.*

BATTLEFIELD ARCHAEOLOGY

Only recently has WWI been seen as worth studying archaeologically. In 2001, a mass grave of twelve German soldiers was uncovered at Gavrelle, France, revealing skeletons still wearing helmets, and apparently hastily buried by their comrades. In Belgian Flanders, in the old Ypres battlefield, local amateur groups carried out excavations until 2002. Then, the Belgian Institute for the Archaeological Heritage of Western Flanders became officially involved. Its first dig was an excavation in the path of a freeway extension outside Ypres. Archaeological reconnaissance included aerial photographs, trench maps, and contemporary accounts of the fighting, as well as interviews of local residents and on-site documentation. This comprehensive approach identified nine zones for investigation and revealed differences between German and British structures. Seven human bodies, trench systems, soldiers' equipment, ammunition, and "duckboards"—long planks used by the soldiers to help them walk across muddy areas—were found. Professional archaeology arrived on the battlefields of the western front in 2002. The most important development that year was the establishment of the first Department of WWI Archaeology in Belgium, which focuses attention on who should be allowed to excavate, how, where, and when.

"Remains unearthed from the fields of Passchendaele provide a timely reminder of the brutality of trench life.

"Yesterday, a few miles north of Ypres, the remains of another nameless British soldier were being unearthed. Not much was left—a few bones, some buttons, and a pair of boots—lying in the crater gouged by the shell that killed him. Over the last few months, a team of British and Belgian archaeologists have been busy excavating a trench system near the village of St. Jan. The site is on the route of a new motorway and the government in Brussels decreed that it should be thoroughly researched. Six British dead have been recovered and, for once, a name may soon be attached to one of them. William Storey was barely a man when he signed up for the Northumberland Fusiliers. From Blyth, Northumberland, he was part of a detachment from the regiment's 5th Battalion, which went into action on October 26, 1917. In all probability he was killed by a shell while waiting to go forward."

Daily Telegraph report, November 11, 2003.

Above: *Items recovered from the battlefields of Flanders by the Institute for the Archaeological Heritage of Western Flanders.*

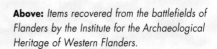

PROTECTING MEMORIES

The excavations of WWI sites may involve events that can, for some descendants of WWI soldiers, conjure up memories. Those who investigate, including the various media, who often highlight images of skeletons of unknown soldiers, must remain sensitive to such family members. After all, thousands of unidentified men could still lie beneath WWI battlefields. In the United States, fewer than fifty WWI veterans—of the nearly 4.5 million who served— were still around to honor Memorial Day in May 2005. The American Battle Monuments Commission, set up by an act of Congress in 1923, honors the sacrifices of all U.S. war dead. The United States also observes a national holiday to honor the Armistice. Now called Veterans Day, it is observed every November 11, and is a nationwide day of respect marked by services at various memorials.

Above: *Belgian archaeologists excavate a serpentine trench at Crossroads Farm, the infamous no-man's-land between the warring forces.*

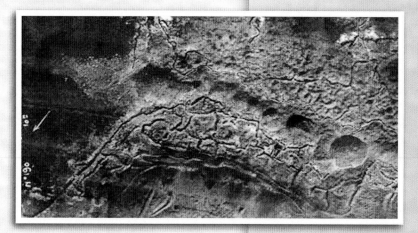

Above: *An aerial photograph taken in no-man's-land clearly reveals WWI trenches.*

TIME LINE
2002–2004

2002
Department of World War I archaeology established in Belgian Flanders.

2004
Professional excavations at Serre, near the Somme.

"Flanders still yields remains.
Shoe and bones of unidentified WWI soldier unearthed in Ypres, Belgium.

"Eighty-five years after the end of World War I, investigators are still finding remains of soldiers who perished in Flanders fields—site of some of the war's most intense fighting. They uncovered the remains of a British soldier Friday, the seventh serviceman found since excavations began a year ago on Pilkem Ridge, where twelve thousand men died in one day in 1917 at the start of the Third Battle of Ypres. In the surrounding area of southwest Belgium, remains belonging to dozens of soldiers are found every year, mostly by farmers at plowing time. 'They call it the harvest of bones,' said Peter Francis of the Commonwealth War Graves Commission, in Maidenhead, England. German and allied armies fought in Flanders for over four years in some of the war's most intensive trench warfare. The slaughter was memorialized in an anguished poem by Canadian army surgeon John McCrae: 'In Flanders fields the poppies blow between the crosses, row on row...'"

CNN Report, Tuesday, November 11, 2003

Two important aspects of the war's major figures were the ages of the generals who fought the battles and the variable quality of the politicians who directed it. Generals and politicians on all sides were caught in the same dilemma: How to fight a twentieth-century, industrialized war with nineteenth-century attitudes, strategies, and tactics. Soldiers, civilians, and politicians alike were forced to accept new war technologies such as machine guns, airplanes, poisonous gases, and massive artillery barrages. Humans had become efficient killers and untold millions suffered or died as a result.

Kaiser Wilhelm II 1859–1941

Trained in the Prussian Army tradition, Wilhelm II became German kaiser (emperor) in 1888. He believed passionately that Germany should become a world power to rival Britain, and supported strengthening the army and navy. He dismissed "Iron Chancellor" Otto von Bismarck in 1890 and appointed his own generals during the war. As the personification of a militarized, imperial Germany, he was forced to abdicate when his army faltered in 1918 and the Armistice was signed. He moved to Doorn, the Netherlands, where he lived the rest of his life.

David Lloyd George 1863–1945

Famous for his oratory, Lloyd George entered politics as a Liberal member of Parliament (MP) in 1890. He served as Chancellor of the Exchequer from 1908 to 1914, and became Minister of Munitions in 1915. He served as prime minister between 1916–1918, during which time he tried in vain to take war policy away from the military. He was particularly critical of Haig's conduct of the battles of the Somme and Passchendaele. Aggressively pro-war, George served a second term as prime minister from 1918 to 1922.

Czar Nicholas II 1868–1918

Czar of all the Russias in 1914, Nicholas II was the autocratic ruler of a sprawling multinational empire of one hundred fifty million people. Shy and unworldly, he ruled over an almost medieval rural society which was unprepared for the outbreak of industrialized war. He failed to inspire leadership or make crucial political changes. In 1917, civil unrest developed into the Russian Revolution. The Czar and his family were murdered a year later.

Thomas Woodrow Wilson 1856–1924

Thomas Woodrow Wilson, born on December 28, 1856, was an American scholar. Passionate about literature and politics, he decided to pursue a career in the latter. Wilson was elected governor of New York in 1910, and U.S. president in 1912. Reelected four years later in the middle of the war, Wilson tried in vain to keep the United States neutral. Provoked by unrestricted submarine warfare and German subterfuge with Mexico, Wilson asked Congress to declare war on Germany in April 1917. He began mobilizing the U.S. Army under General John Pershing. After the war, Wilson negotiated successfully for the creation of the League of Nations. Despite his efforts, he lost the 1920 presidential election by a landslide.

Lord Kitchener of Khartoum 1850–1916

Kitchener was sixty-four in 1914 when he became British secretary of state for war. He began his army career in the Royal Engineers and rose to prominence in one of Britain's many colonial conflicts in Africa. He was made a lord after helping to successfully repel anticolonialist forces in Sudan, Africa. His most important contribution was the recognition of the need for a large volunteer force to reinforce the small professional army of the time. Millions responded to the call and joined the so-called Kitchener Army thanks to the famous "Your Country Needs You!" poster showing Kitchener's face and a pointing finger. He died unexpectedly in 1916 en route to Russia when his ship, the HMS *Hampshire*, hit a mine in the Baltic Sea.

General Paul von Hindenburg 1847–1934

Hindenburg was sixty-six years old in 1914. He was brought out of retirement to successfully command the German Eighth Army on the eastern front between 1914 and 1916. Hero status followed, and he was appointed chief of staff in 1916. He helped end the slaughter at Verdun and built the defensive Hindenburg Line (*Siegfried Stellung*). The failure of his spring 1918 offensive led to the armistice of November 11. Despite this defeat, Hindenburg became president of the Weimar Republic in 1925. Hindenburg is infamous for his fateful decision to appoint Nazi leader Adolf Hitler as chancellor of Germany in 1933—a decision that helped propel the world into another global conflict. Hindenburg died in 1934.

Douglas, First Earl Haig (Field Marshal Lord) Haig 1861-1928

Haig is arguably the most controversial British military figure of WWI. He was the classic example of a professional cavalry officer whose ideas and tactics belonged to small-scale nineteenth-century colonial conflicts. Before WWI, Haig served in India, South Africa, and the Sudan, Africa. He was eventually appointed director of military training at the War Office in 1906. Despite this record, Haig was slow to adapt to the dramatically changed circumstances of industrialized war fought by trench-bound infantry. His inefficiencies resulted in the terrible losses of British soldiers during the battles of the Somme (1916) and Passchendaele (1917). He persevered and learned from his mistakes, taking his forces to final victory in 1918.

General Joseph Jacques Joffre 1852–1931

Joseph Joffre (*on left in photo*) was of humble origin, but rose to become the dominant French figure in WWI until 1916. He served in the Franco-Prussian war in 1870–1871, as well as in several colonial campaigns, and also worked as a military engineer. By the time WWI broke out, Joffre was sixty-three years old. He became commander in chief of the French army. General Joffre successfully stopped the German advance at the First Battle of the Marne in September 1914. He then played a less active role in the war. In 1916, after the Battle of Verdun, he was removed from office.

General Henri–Philippe Petain 1856–1951

Compared to other generals of the time, Henri-Philippe Pétain used cautious tactics that advocated the strategy of strong defense rather than endless and costly infantry attacks. He put this into practice at Verdun in 1916. In 1917, aged sixty-one, Pétain was appointed commander in chief of the French army, replacing General Nivelle. Pétain became a controversial figure during World War II, governing Nazi-occupied France under the Vichy regime for the Germans. During this time, he was implicated in the deportation of many French Jews to their deaths. Although sentenced to death in 1945, French president Charles de Gaulle commuted Pétain's sentence to life in prison.

General John J. ("Black Jack") Pershing 1860–1948

In April 1917, West Point graduate John J. Pershing became the World War I commander of the American Expeditionary Force (AEF) in Europe. He increased the size of the U.S. Army from about 25,000 troops to nearly three million in a little over a year. Pershing earned his nickname during the 1890s while assigned to a "Buffalo Soldiers" unit of black men in the 10th Cavalry. Afterward, he championed the rights of all-black units to participate fully in all aspects of military endeavors. Pershing served as leader in the successful Meuse-Argonne offensive battle of 1918. His 1931 autobiography, *My Experience of War*, won the Pulitzer Prize for history in 1932. Pershing died on July 15, 1948.

General Erich von Ludendorff 1856–1937

In 1914, von Ludendorff served as quartermaster general of the German Second Army. His qualities as a tactician led to the successful invasion of Belgium and particularly the capture of Liège. As chief of staff to Hindenburg, he mobilized Germany for total war and initiated the controversial policy of unrestricted submarine warfare, which convinced the U.S. to enter the war. After the German defeat, von Ludendorff moved to Sweden, where he became a writer, lauding the abilities of the vanquished German forces. Ludendorff returned to Germany in the 1920s, where he took part in Hitler's failed Nazi rising in Munich. Despite this, he continued to represent the Nazis and served in the Reichstag from 1924 to 1928. He died in 1937; Adolf Hitler was among the mourners.

Marshal Ferdinand Foch 1851–1929

Ferdinand Foch (on right) served in the Franco-Prussian War and developed a reputation for expertise in artillery tactics. Foch played a crucial role in achieving French success at the First Battle of the Marne in 1914. His greatest achievement, however, lay in becoming the first commander in chief of all Allied armies in March 1918. With the strong-willed generals Haig, Pétain, and Pershing under his authority, Foch devised and carried out a successful grand strategy that led to German capitulation in November 1918. Foch was greatly praised and decorated by the victorious nations after WWI. Foch warned that the harsh terms of Versailles would lead to future trouble. He died in 1929.

GLOSSARY

Allies Britain, France, Russia, Belgium, Serbia, Italy, Japan, China, and the United States.

ANZAC acronym applied for the armed forces of Australia and New Zealand.

annexation the addition of territory.

aristocracy a social upper class that often governed countries in Europe.

Armistice the formal agreement that ended WWI on November 11, 1918.

attrition strategy employed by both sides to weaken and exhaust resources of men and matériel with continuous attacks.

battalion unit of infantry in an army, made of two or more companies and about one thousand troops.

"bite-and-hold" strategy involving attacking, winning, and then consolidating the enemy's trenches, often provoking counterattacks.

brigade unit of an army division made of four to six battalions.

British Expeditionary Force (BEF) term originally given to the six British divisions sent to France in 1914 and later to all the armies of the British Empire serving in France.

capitulated stopped resisting a situation or set of proposed terms; surrendered.

casualites wounds or deaths caused by armed conflict; can refer to the military or civilians.

Central Powers German Empire, Austro-Hungarian Empire, Turkey, and Bulgaria.

company unit of infantry battalion; between one hundred fifty and two hundred fifty troops.

conscription forced service in the military.

demilitarization the removal or reduction of military forces from an area or country.

demobilization the dismantling of army units and the return of soldiers to civilian life.

dogfights intense aerial battles, usually in small planes and often in tight airspace.

duckboards long boards placed over muddy areas to ease access.

Hindenburg Line (*Siegfried Stellung*) defensive line of barbed wire, trenches, and fortifications built by the Germans in France.

Hindenburg Plan a plan that put the entire German economy under government control.

legacy attitudes, situations, or material possessions left by a predecessor.

League of Nations international organization of sovereign countries set up during the interwar years to keep the peace and settle disputes through negotiation; precursor to the United Nations.

logistics support system of matériel and services given to armies to keep them effective as fighting forces.

matériel equipment and supplies used for military purposes.

mobilization process of calling up the reserves of the armed forces to maximize military strength.

munitions mainly refers to artillery shells and rifle and machine-gun bullets.

no-man's-land the dangerous unclaimed area between opposing sides.

noncombatant individual whose wartime duties excluded fighting.

propaganda selective broadcast of information designed to influence public opinion.

reconnaissance the gathering of military information, such as troop strength and location.

Reichstag the elected legislative body of Germany.

reign a time span of royal authority.

reparations compensation payments by a defeated country for damage inflicted by war.

salient a battle line of one force that projects into or beyond an enemy's battle line.

Schlieffen Plan German military plan by Alfred von Schlieffen designed to defeat French forces in the west before Russia could mobilize in the east.

shell-shock combat fatigue characterized by mental exhaustion and confusion; often caused by sustained exposure to shelling.

shrapnel weapon fragments designed to inflict serious injury or death.

strategy overall plan for the large-scale conduct of war.

tactics methods for carrying out strategies.

tinderbox a situation with the high probability of changing into an explosive, violent event.

Tirpitz Plan plan devised by Admiral Tirpitz to make Germany into a major naval power to rival the United Kingdom's Royal Navy.

total war the militarization and dedication of an entire country's economy and resources to a war.

Treaty of Versailles peace treaty, signed on June 28, 1919, that brought WWI to an official end and spelled out Germany's punishment.

trench art objects made by soldiers and civilians from recycled war scraps.

troop one soldier.

troops a group of soldiers.

truce a temporary or permanent cease-fire agreement between warring sides.

Weimar Republic the democratic government of Germany after 1918 that took its name from the town of Weimar, where it was originally based.

zeppelins football-shaped airships used in WWI combat and reconnaissance missions.

Please visit our web site at: www.garethstevens.com
For a free color catalog describing Gareth Stevens Publishing's
list of high-quality books and multimedia programs,
call 1-800-542-2595 or 1-800-387-3178 (Canada).
Gareth Stevens Publishing's fax: (414) 332-3567.

Library of Congress Cataloging-in-Publication Data

Saunders, Nicholas.
    World War I: a primary source history / Nicholas Saunders.
        p. cm. — (In their own words)
    Includes bibliographical references and index.
    ISBN 0-8368-5982-0 (lib. bdg.)
    1. World War, 1914-1918—Juvenile literature. I. Title:
World War One. II. Title: World War 1. III. Title.
    IV. In their own words (Milwaukee, Wis.)
    D522.7.S38   2005
    940.3—dc22   2005044243

This North American edition first published in 2006 by
Gareth Stevens Publishing
A Member of the WRC Media Family of Companies
330 West Olive Street, Suite 100
Milwaukee, WI 53212 USA

This U.S. edition copyright © 2006 by Gareth Stevens, Inc.
Original edition copyright © 2005 ticktock Entertainment Ltd.
First published in Great Britain in 2005 by ticktock Media Ltd.,
Unit 2, Orchard Business Centre, North Farm Road,
Tunbridge Wells, Kent, TN2 3XF, U.K.

Gareth Stevens editor: Carol Ryback
Gareth Stevens art direction: Tammy West
Gareth Stevens designer: Jenni Gaylord

Photo credits (b=bottom; c=center; l=left; r=right; t=top)
Alamy: 22(b), 23(t). Art Archive: 5(tr), 6(b), 17(br), 30(all), 32(t), 33(t).
CORBIS: 5(br), 6-7(b), 7(b), 8(t), 11(t), 16(c), 17(c), 24(c), 25(b),
28–29(b), 38–39(all). Everett Collection: 31(all). Getty Images: 12(c),
(13r). Imperial War Museum: 10–11(b). Mary Evans Picture Library:
8–9(c), 10(t), 10(cl), Library of Congress: 43(t).

Every effort has been made to trace the copyright holders. We apologize
in advance for any unintentional omissions. We would be pleased to
insert the appropriate acknowledgments in any subsequent edition of
this publication.

Printed in the United States of America

1 2 3 4 5 6 7 8 9 09 08 07 06 05